The Last Elephant

Lee Craker

Copyright © 2014 Lee Craker

All rights reserved.

ISBN: 1495375730
ISBN-13: 978-1495375736

DEDICATION

This book is dedicated to my beautiful wife Jang, my daughter Gammy, the people of Thailand, and all people everywhere who care about the welfare of elephants.

CONTENTS

	Acknowledgments	i
	Forward	Pg # 1
1	Symbol of a Nation	Pg # 5
2	The Road to Chiang Rai	Pg # 11
3	The Golden Triangle Asian Elephant Foundation	Pg # 15
4	The Elephant Photographer	Pg # 21
5	Rumble in the Jungle	Pg # 25
6	Maesa Elephant Camp	Pg # 33
7	The Chiang Mai Zoo	Pg # 46
8	Elephant Nature Park / Lek Chailert	Pg # 50
9	How to Help the Elephants	Pg # 60

ACKNOWLEDGMENTS

This book would not be possible without the support and help of many people. I am indebted to George Merkert, Lek Chailert, Dan Bucknell, Carol Stevenson and John Roberts for their help and support. I also want to thank the people of Thailand for their generous hospitality, and to many others along this journey.

FORWARD

My first encounter with an elephant was as a young man, when I spent a summer working at Cheyenne Mountain Zoo in Colorado Springs, Colorado. Among my many duties was to assist in giving elephant rides. I would help people onto the elephants back from a platform, and the keeper would walk Kimba, the elephant, around in a circle. My mind was mostly occupied with safety concerns, and I did not really get to know Kimba that well, but I could see there was a bond between her and her keeper, Ron. I learned how deep the bond was during en episode that took place that summer. The zoo was undergoing some construction, and care was taken so that the heavy machinery was not used while Kimba was walking from her cage or giving rides, so as not to frighten her. One morning a new caterpillar driver started to work unaware of the rules and drove a very large backhoe into the elephant rides area while Kimba was working. This large, loud machine must have looked like a fierce animal to Kimba, who reacted in a defensive manner and was set to attack what she thought, was a large aggressive animal. I grabbed the child I had just placed on Kimba's back as the scene started to unfold and climbed down from my tower and ran towards the back hoe shouting to the driver: "turn it off, turn it off." The expression on the drivers face was one of surprise and wide eyed fear. He shut the Cat down and ran down the path away from the trumpeting, agitated elephant. Ron, Kimba's keeper, in the mean time, had taken a position in front of Kimba, her trunk on his chest. To reach the back hoe, Kimba would have had to run over Ron. Ron never lost his composure, talking calmly to Kimba and maneuvering his body to be in between Kimba and the fearsome machine. It was an amazing scene. Kimba with no restraints what so ever, towered over Ron her keeper, but refused to hurt Ron or throw him out of her way. Ron was able to calm Kimba down and they both left for her cage at the other end of the zoo, in a fast trot. I followed to see if I could help get people out of the way if needed. When we arrived at the cage Kimba shared with her sister Lucy, the other workers were in a near panic. Lucy had heard Kimba's cries, even though the rides area was a mile away, and she was going to tear down her cage to go and help Kimba. She was straining at her chains with her trunk around the bars trying to rip the door from the cage. Upon seeing Kimba, Lucy calmed down and peace was restored. From this episode I learned that elephants have strong family ties, and can communicate over long distances. I also learned that even as frightened as Kimba was, she would do nothing that would harm her trainer Ron.

That summer at the zoo was educational in many ways. I developed a deep respect for the keepers, who truly did love the animals, and I began to share their distain for cages. The keepers more than anyone, disliked seeing a wild animal in a cage, and yet their love for the animals kept them from walking away, most had worked at the zoo for many years, caring for the animals. I became very close to a Siberian tiger that summer and hated to see him in a cage. I used to day dream about helping him escape, but it was only a dream, for in reality if he did ever escape he would stand a good chance of being killed or injured. In a way my zoo experience gave me a background for what I was to learn and experience here in Thailand.

This book can be summed up in one sentence. Elephant abuse is caused by lack of education. You see, I believe that the consumer controls the product. I believe that the power to change the world for the better is in the hands of the people. Elephant abuse will stop when it is no longer profitable. I also have a fundamental belief in the goodness of people. I believe if you educate people they will make good and intelligent choices. It is the uneducated that make poor choices, and in the case of elephants it is this ignorance that causes elephant abuse and puts money in the pockets of the abusers. The solution to the elephant abuse problem is not in the hands of any government that only complicates the issues, especially in Thailand. The reaction I often hear from westerners is that laws should be passed, or enforced. Thailand is a county with many laws, but few are enforced. There are laws on the books that address almost all of the issues in this book. For reasons too numerous to list here, the laws are not, and will not be enforced. The true solution is through education.

The ultimate goal of this book is to make Thailand a better place for elephants, and thus for visitors, which will ultimately benefit the Thai people. I make my home in Thailand, and I have found, the common people, the farmers, police, government officials, and so many others to be kind and wonderful people. Thailand is truly the land of smiles.

That is not to say Thailand does not have a dark side. Every culture on earth has a dark side. Every country can be improved. I hope this book can be seen in that light. I want to applaud the good, and try to improve what is wrong.

1 SYMBOL OF A NATION

The elephant has long been associated with Thailand. For centuries the elephant was the national symbol of Siam; used to fight wars, laboring in agriculture and industry, and revered by the country's 65 million Buddhists. So powerful is the elephant as a symbol in Thailand that it is believed the wellbeing and prosperity of the Kingdom is linked to the number of "white" elephants in the royal stables.

For longer than anyone can remember, elephants have been part of the culture and folklore of Thailand. Everywhere you look in Thailand you will see an elephant. Elephant figures are carved into buildings, statues of elephants can be found in every city, elephant tusks are used in the temples, there is elephant jewelry in almost every boutique and countless products are named after the elephant. Just as the bald eagle is easily recognized as the symbol of America, after a visit to Thailand, the elephant will always remind you of the land of smiles.

One may wonder how reverence and abuse can co-exist side by side. Part of the problem is by no means unique to Thailand. Many cultures the world over share a history of disregard for the animal kingdom and also share the guilt of centuries of animal abuse. It is only very recently that animals in some countries are considered to have rights. Only in the last few years have we come to understand that so much of what we once considered only human traits we share with elephants. We now understand that elephants have feelings, morn the loss of loved ones, can communicate with each other over vast distances and have strong family units. They are creatures like us. Before this understanding and a shift in the way we as humans view the animal world, it was considered natural to use elephants to do the work that was difficult or dangerous for humans, it was commonplace to inflict pain so that the elephant obeyed commands and it was accepted that the way to tame elephants was through a horrific process called the "crush". The way elephants are "broken" and trained has remained the same for centuries. The new idea that this pain need not be inflicted on a baby elephant in the learning process is foreign to those that make their living by trading in baby elephants. And the idea that elephants should not be captured at all is a concept that is beyond comprehension for those who live in poverty and who make a meager living from capturing baby elephants.

Those of us that agree with this new way of looking at the animal world can pat ourselves on the back for helping to start a shift in global animal rights conciseness, we must be aware however, that there are millions of those who do not share our views. My friends, the work has only just begun.

On April 5th, 2013 it was reported that the last Vietnamese wild elephant had been killed near Quang Binh in Vietnam. International Business Times: *"An elephant believed to be the last one living in the wilds of the north-central province of Quang Binh in Vietnam has been found dead. The animal had its head, tusks, tail and skin cut off, and had been disemboweled, the Tuoi Tre newspaper said. Dihn Quy Nhan, chairman of the Minh Hoa District People's Committee, told the online newspaper Dan Tri that experts believe the animal had died two days before locals found it. The corpse had started to decompose when it was found in the Tan Hoa Commune forest. Authorities say they do not know why the elephant had been skinned and beheaded. However, Vietnam is known for its ivory trade and many parts are used for decoration or in traditional medicine. The WWF says Vietnam is one of the worst countries for ivory trade in the world."*

According to Scientific American, 100 elephants are being killed daily in Africa. It is my reluctant belief that the African elephant will probably become extinct in our lifetimes. I hope I'm wrong, but the facts and figures are all pointing to the conclusion that the African elephant is on it's last legs as a species. Unless meaningful action is taken right away, the Asian elephant will soon follow.

One hundred years ago there were an estimated 100,000 Asian elephants in Thailand. Today, their numbers have declined to estimates of between 3,500 to 5,000 due to a multitude of threats, ranging from the desire for ivory, the destruction of forest habitat to make way for farming and the massacre of elephants that is a by-product of the capture and domestication of wild baby elephants to supply elephant tourism. The notion of elephant extinction is no longer just a concern; it is the new reality.

Thailand's tradition of legally using elephants in industry ended in 1989 following the catastrophic floods in Thailand that in part, were an outcome of irresponsible logging. The government's cancellation of logging concessions put thousands of elephants, and the mahouts who owned them, out of work. The mahouts had few options to support their families or feed their elephants, which can consume up to 440 lb. of food a day. Many mahouts fled to cities with their elephants to beg, while others turned to illegal logging or resorted to elephant tourism. The tourist industry is the newest contributor to the demise of the Thai elephant. Elephant camps cater to tourists and use elephants irresponsibly, forcing them to provide rides in a cruel manner, in adverse weather and perform gymnastic displays for "entertainment." City life is debilitating for elephants. They are used to beg from tourists and are subjected to severe cruelty. On the streets elephants are forced to walk with their sensitive foot pads on hot asphalt and concrete, there is no dirt to spray themselves with for protection from the sun, clean water is rare and they are forced to drink from public fountains, standards of health are low, drugging with amphetamines is common, the hours of work are long, diet is poor, and road accidents involving elephants are frequent.

For elephants to work in this multi million-dollar industry, baby elephants are prematurely separated from their mothers, who are killed in the process. Their life expectancy is reduced to as little as five years due to stress, malnutrition, and other threats. Baby elephants are one of the newest and most popular attractions for tourism and to meet the demand, forced breeding under harsh conditions often occurs, they are captured in the wild illegally in Thailand or brought across the border from Burma.

Illegal logging bodes just as poorly for elephants. Animals are pumped with amphetamines to increase work time and suppress appetites. Elephants are often beaten and starved to ensure compliancy. Illegal logging is carried out along the Thai-Burma border where there is a long history of war. Consequently, live land mines still exist and countless cases of elephant maiming and deaths are reported. The well being of the elephants are not the owners priorities, but sadly money is. If there is a consistent theme when it comes to elephant abuse, that common ground would be greed. African elephants are being slaughtered by the thousands for one thing only, ivory, and Asian elephants are being captured, tortured, and killed to line the pockets of a few wealthy individuals.

The Last Elephant

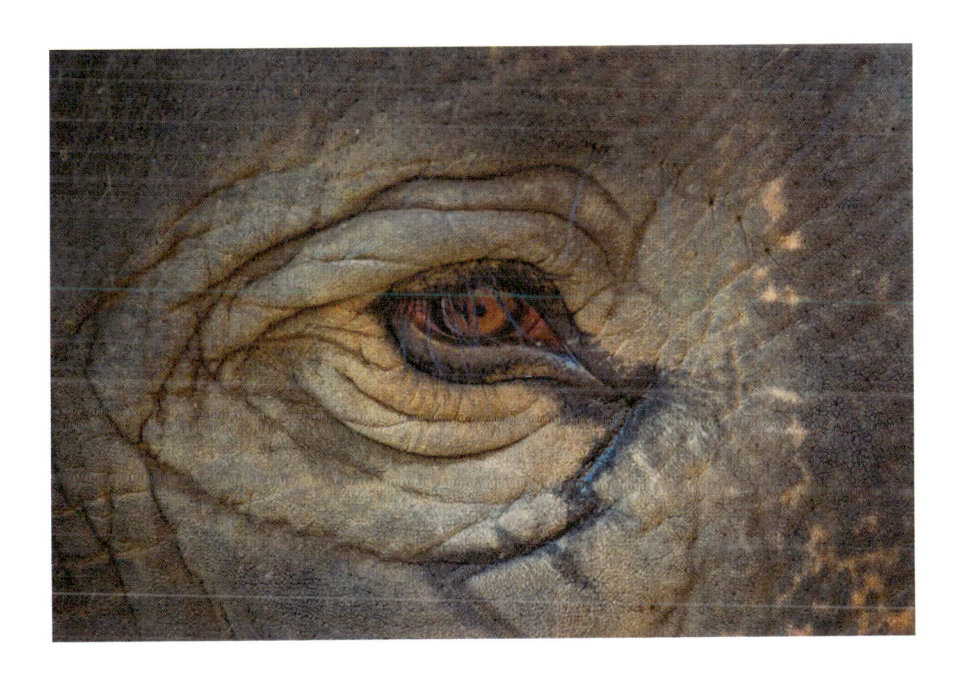

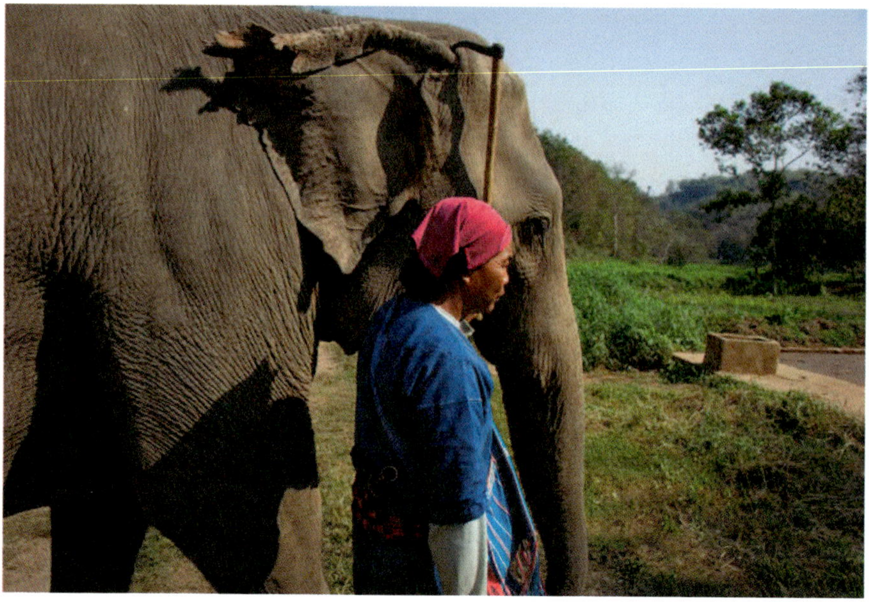

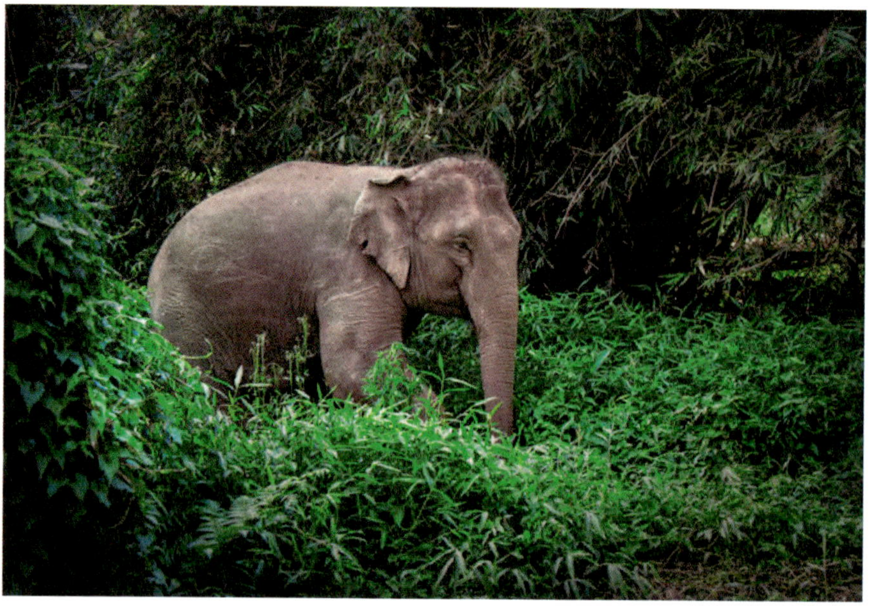

2 THE ROAD TO CHIANG RAI

My heightened awareness of elephant issues, and hence this book can be attributed to conversations with a good friend, George Merkert, in early 2012. George is in the film industry, and is a concerned advocate on behalf of many important issues. George and I started talking about the ivory problem in Africa and how inconceivable it was that elephants might become extinct in our lifetime simply because of the world's demand for ivory. Our early conversations centered on the ivory trade and Thailand's role as the second largest importer of raw ivory behind China. At that time George was unaware of what I thought was an issue just as important as the ivory trade, and that was the live elephant trade in Thailand. I explained that the animal rights world is focusing on Africa and ivory, which is a good thing, and indeed a worthy cause, but the live elephant trade in Thailand is also worthy of our attention. Due to the fact that the Asian elephant numbers are substantially less than the African species, if everything remains the same, the Asian elephant may become extinct even before the African elephant, and if not, will surely become extinct shortly afterword, unless things change.

As our conversations on this issue became more frequent I started doing intensive research on the live elephant problem in Thailand. The more I researched the more I realized that I must see and photograph elephant camps in Thailand.

I wanted to approach the subject by taking a look at the problems, and also what is being done to address the issues and help the elephants of Thailand. I wanted to use this angle for my story because there have been many documentaries done on the capture of baby elephants and the "crush", the horrific method of breaking the elephant's spirit and domesticating the elephant. Also I have lived in Thailand just over three years and can remember vividly my own experiences with elephants when I came to Thailand as a tourist before making my home in Thailand. I had a vision that if I were to make a difference as a journalist, I need to make people aware of the problems and then give them an alternative to unknowingly supporting elephant abuse when they visit Thailand.

Oh, what a can of worms I opened! I found there are literally hundreds of elephant camps in Thailand. Most say exactly the same thing in their advertising, they are helping the poor elephants, giving them a better life and for a couple of thousand baht you can interact with these magnificent creatures. My initial discovery was not unexpected; the elephant trade in Thailand is big business. In a country where money is all-important, elephants are certainly one of Thailand top attractions. Just how important elephant tourism is can be seen by the way in which the government promotes it. The Tourism Authority of Thailand advertises and supports elephant tourism almost as vigorously as they promote human trafficking which they call "sex tourism", which is arguably Thailand's number one tourist attraction, rivaling the sales of counterfeit goods and intellectual rights theft.

After I made the decision to visit elephant camps the question became how do I choose which camps to visit? I sent many e-mails and carefully read the numerous responses. I did follow-up e-mails explaining I was a journalist, and this time the responses were quite few. It became clear that most camps were not open to having a documentary photographer as a guest. I made sure that a couple of the camps that did not want journalistic scrutiny would be on my list to visit. Of the responses I received, two camps peaked my interest the most. One simply stated, "we are the best". I like that. I like someone with courage that say we are the best, come visit, and see for yourself. So I did.

It became increasing clear in my research that North Thailand in the areas of Chiang Mai and Chiang Rai with their numerous elephant camps and close proximity to the Myanmar/Burma border was going to give me the best opportunity to learn about the elephant situation in Thailand. In my correspondence I had the opportunity to talk with and do a voice interview on SKYPE with Dan Bucknell of Elephant Family Org. Dan was very helpful and parts of Dan's interview are in a report I did for CNN. Dan was instrumental in educating me on the elephant situation in Thailand. Until I spoke with Dan at length, I was thinking my story was going to partly be about the illegal ivory trade in Thailand. I became convinced that although the ivory trade is a big problem worldwide, there is pressing problem locally, here in Thailand, with the live elephant trade. I have always believed that I should concentrate my efforts where they would do the most good, and in the case of the live elephant trade and abuse here in Thailand the problem is in my back yard so to speak, giving me the opportunity to investigate as a local rather than a foreigner, and use the skills of my wife as an interpreter. Dan is located in England making a visit to chat with him in person impractical, but Dan introduced me to John Edward Roberts of The Golden Triangle Asian Elephant Foundation, near Chiang Rai. I was impressed with both John Roberts and Lek Chailert of Elephant Nature Park located near Chiang Mai. So with my decision made I was off to North Thailand to discover what I could about the elephant camps in Thailand.

I spent 4 weeks in Chiang Mai and Chiang Rai, Thailand visiting 3 elephant camps and a zoo. I had a chance to visit those who were fighting an uphill battle in elephant conversation and rescue, and I also saw the abusers.

3 THE GOLDEN TRIANGLE ASIAN ELEPHANT FOUNDATION

From opium to elephants.
The Anantara Golden Triangle resort is located in the lush rolling hills near the town of Golden Triangle, Thailand. The Golden Triangle area earned it's name from the opium business. The Golden Triangle was (and is) one of Asia's two main opium-producing areas. It is an area of around 367,000 square miles that overlaps the mountains of four countries of Southeast Asia: Myanmar, Vietnam, Laos and Thailand. Countless millions have been made in this area by supplying opium to the world. It would be impossible to count the number of lives destroyed by the opium produced in the Golden Triangle and almost as difficult to count the number of millionaires this area has produced. This is the backdrop for Anantara, a 4 star hotel and resort located a short distance from the town of Golden Triangle. What makes Anantara's resort unique is not the dark world of illegal drugs however, it is elephants. The resort is home to Anantara's Golden Triangle Elephant Camp. Here elephants that have been rescued from the streets or logging concerns and their mahouts are given shelter, and a livelihood. So popular is the elephant resort that *Complex City Guide* listed Anantara Golden Triangle as #12 in their Hotels You Need to Have Sex in Before You Die section. They say: "... *you can impress you sex toy with that knowledge (elephant knowledge) as you ride these elephants through the hills of Laos and Myanmar at the gorgeously exotic Anantara Golden Triangle Elephant Camp and Resort.*"

So the day after I left my humble home in Nakhon Nayok, Thailand, with my shy Thai wife, I find myself having morning coffee overlooking a vast area of jungle and river in a hotel that is known for it's aphrodisiac properties, and occasionally wondering *"how do I get myself into these situations?"*

The day before, shortly after we arrived at Anantara's I had taken a tour. I spent part of the afternoon observing a Target Training Workshop Anantara was hosting. The idea behind Target Training is to teach animals to obey commands without abuse or pain. I spoke with Dr. Gerardo Martinez, who travels the world teaching Target Training not only to elephant handlers, but to anyone who works with animals. The elephants are put behind a cage like partition and then on command move their bodies to touch a "Target" which is a stick with a bright colored cloth held by their mahout. Then they are rewarded for their obedience by being given elephant treats to eat.

It has been several months since I witnessed this training, and now that time has passed I am impressed with the training, and I also applaud John Roberts and staff for putting on the workshop. But I did not feel that way at first. Back then I was a rookie in the elephant world and my thoughts were, "*this is fine and dandy but why? Why are we training elephants? They should be free. Capturing elephants is wrong, capital "W" Wrong. These people just don't get it,*" I thought.

It takes time for someone like myself, who is an idealist, to accept the fact that elephant domestication, and working elephants are not going away. The stakes are too high, the players are too powerful, and the issues are too complicated. So rather than spend time and energy screaming at the top of my lungs saying "this is wrong" and getting nowhere, it is better to support those who are making life a little better for domesticated elephants. I found that John Roberts the founder of Anantara's Golden Triangle Elephant Camp had traveled the same path, philosophically. John believes that elephants belong in the wild, but also realizes that domestic elephants are here to stay, so his work is dedicated to making life better for elephants by rescuing them from the streets and logging camps.

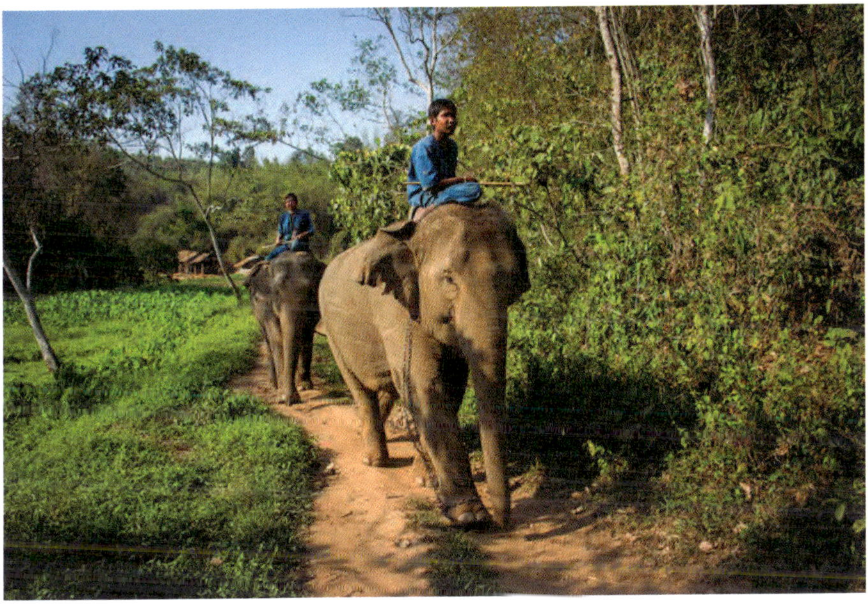

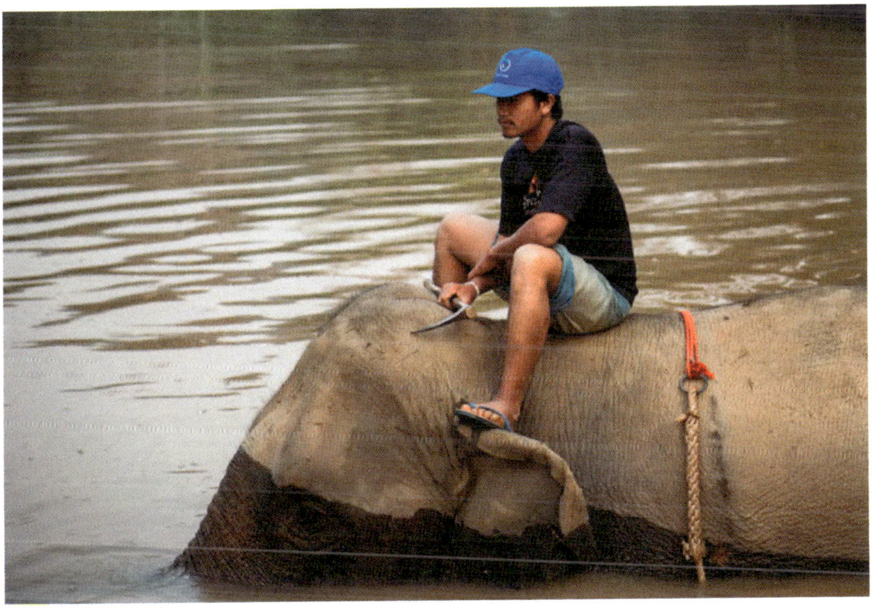

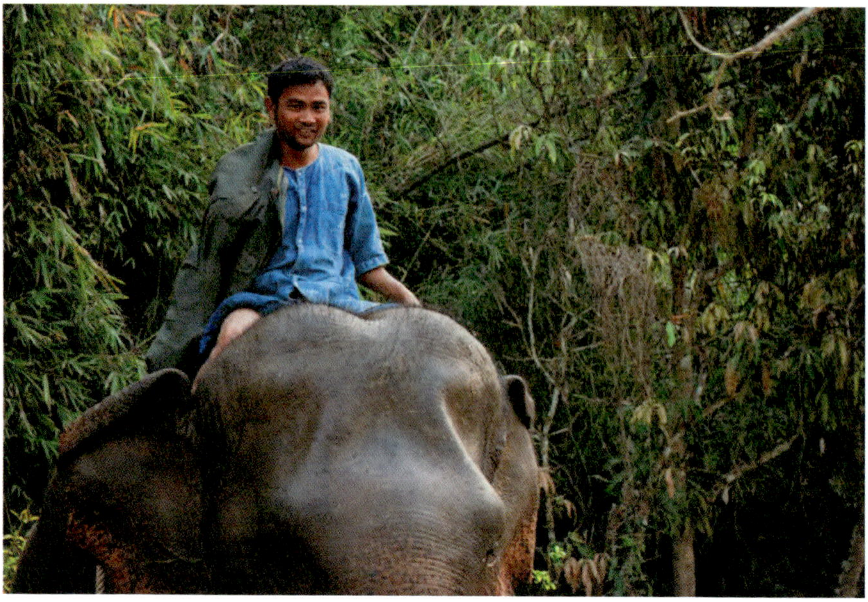

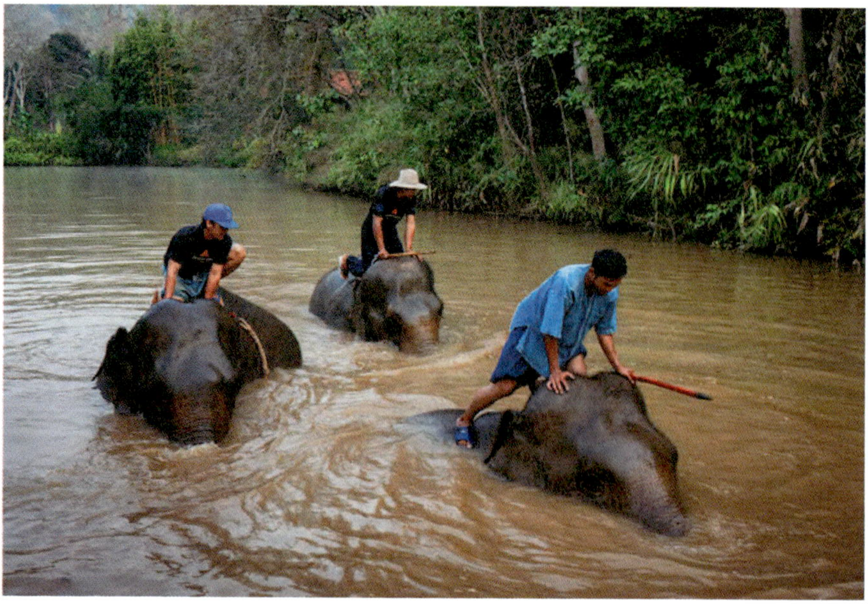

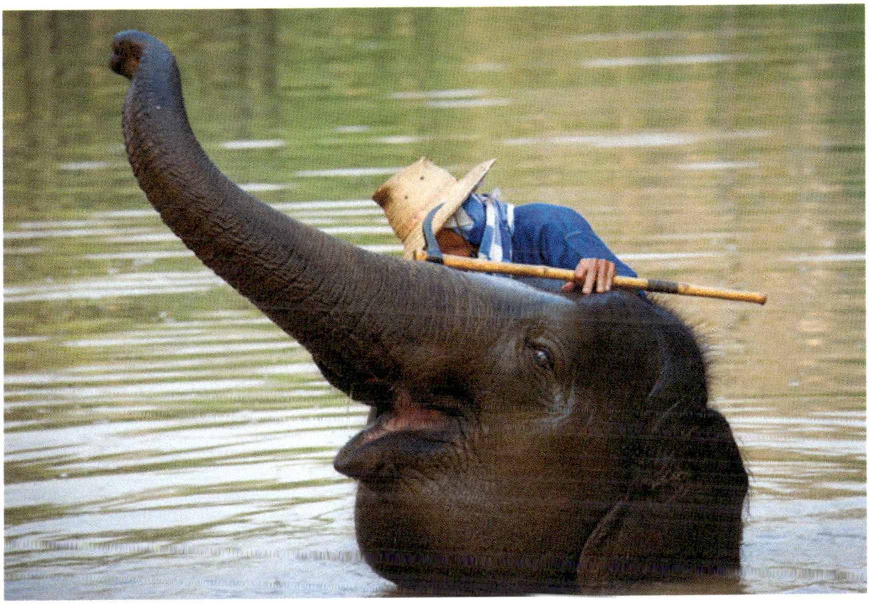

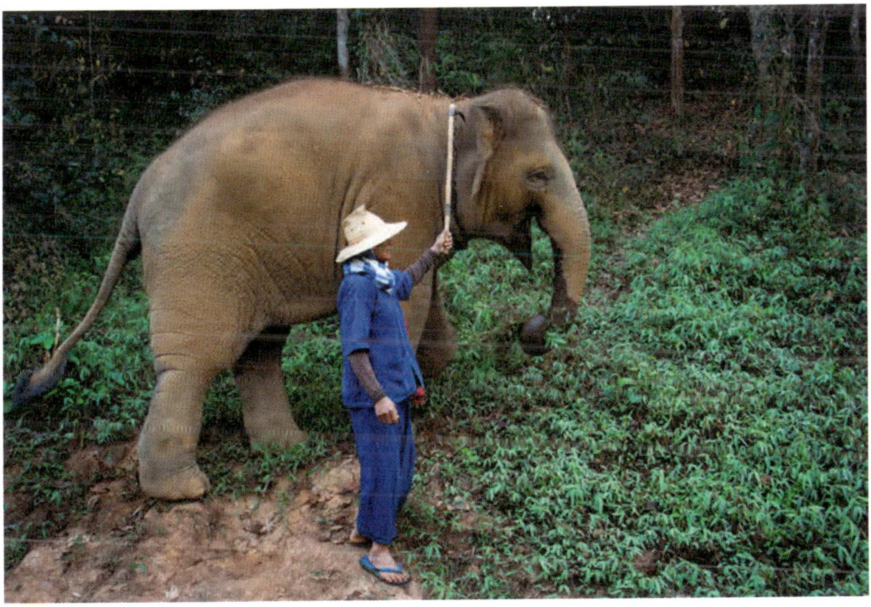

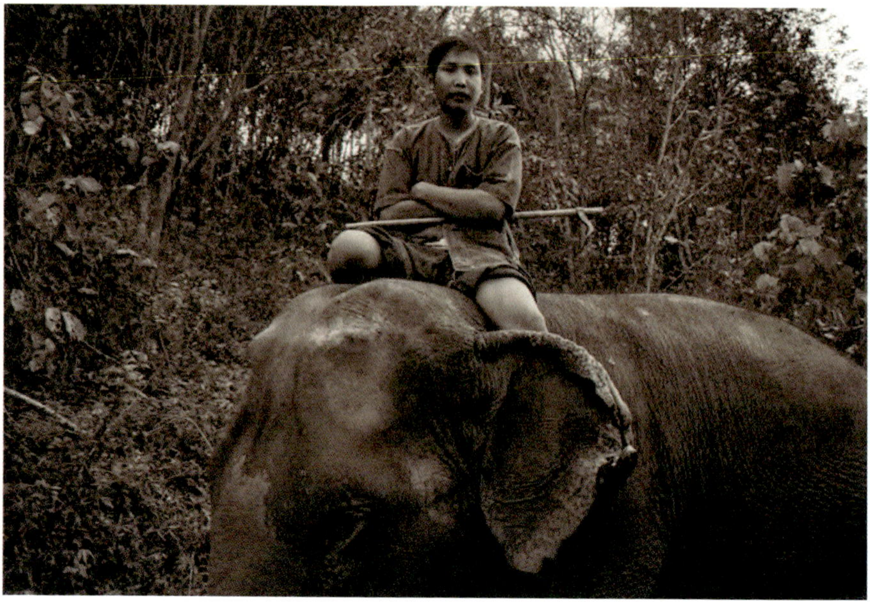

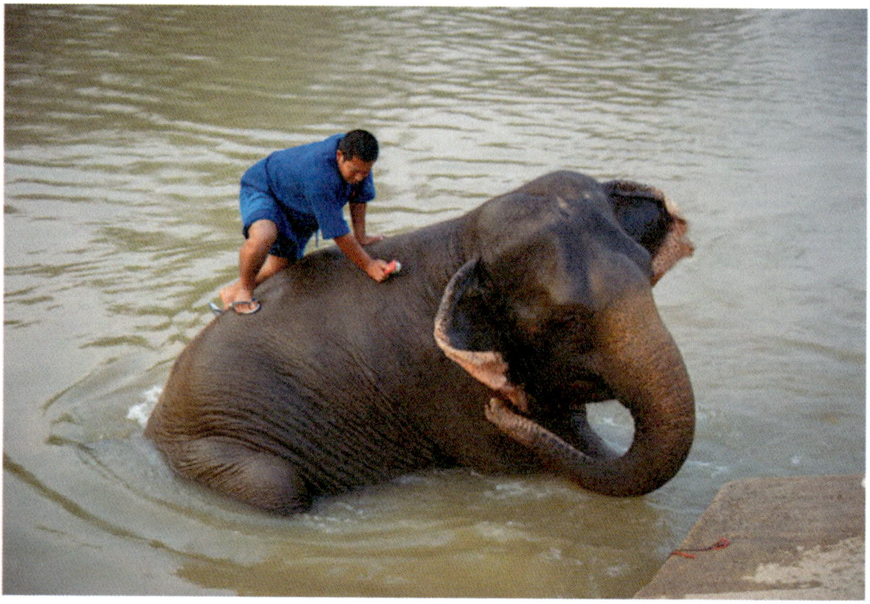

4 THE ELEPHANT PHOTOGRAPHER

As I was having coffee on the deck of Anantara's that first morning I made acquaintances with a fellow photographer. Carol Stevenson. As we shared coffee, and spoke of our backgrounds, I found that Carol had devoted more than 5 years photographing elephants, mostly at Anantara's, and had through her work had gained quite of bit of notoriety and international recognition. Her portraits of elephants and mahouts using a make-shift studio in the jungle are quite good. She has gained the sponsorship of both Nikon Camera and Lowepro Bags. Carol has worked long and hard in elephant rescue and conservation, and a portion of the proceeds from her print sales are given to help the elephants of Thailand, and help support The Golden Triangle Asian Elephant Foundation.

Carol was a wealth of information, and through her, partly because we both speak the same languages, English and Photography, I was able to put together many pieces of the complex Thai elephant puzzle.

It was through Carol that I first learned of the complex and sometimes-turbulent relationships between the various elephant help groups in Thailand. Having worked with charitable organizations in the past, it was easy for me to understand the competition that comes from charities and other help groups having to compete for limited funds and donors.

The disagreements between the elephant rescue and conservation groups in Thailand mostly come from philosophical disagreements over how the rescued elephants are cared for, how to effectively keep the elephants and mahouts off the streets and out of the logging and tourist industries. Disagreements arise over the use of Bull hooks, the proper method of acquiring elephants - purchasing or leasing an elephant - to breed or not to breed, the care of mahouts and their families and much more. It would be nice if the elephant camps that share similar philosophies and goals were to join together in some sort of loose coalition educating tourists and fighting for the elephants. I don't foresee this happening in the near future, leaving those who are preparing to visit Thailand to do their own research, if they plan on visiting an elephant camp.

Recently the issues have become even more complicated as elephant tourism becomes more popular. As I stated above, elephant tourism is big business, and the trend right now is to appeal to the animal rights people or at least to those who care about elephants well being. Because of this there are many more elephant camps that are now advertising they are elephant rescue and conversation camps. I have visited some that are flat out lying. In my mind you can't say you are concerned with an elephant's well being and have the animal play soccer, perform circus tricks and force the animal to trek with several 200 lb. humans in a huge heavy seat and be concerned with anything but profit from elephant tourism.

The reason these circus camps are so successful is lack of education. The average tourist is not aware of how these animals came to be in a camp in the first place, and they do not know what is and what is not cruelty. One would think that knowing what is cruel to an elephant would be fairly obvious, but it is not. The tourist companies over time have done a wonderful job of propagating myths that people believe without question. One myth is that elephants choose to be with people, they would rather be with a human performing tricks than tramping around in the forest munching on veggies and making baby elephants, in fact there is probably a waiting list that elephants sign up for in the jungle and patiently wait to be chained and put in slavery serving humans for the rest of their lives. The truth is my friends, elephants are fierce wild animals, they are willing fight to the death to keep from being captured and they do fight to the death to try and keep their babies from being captured. Think about that the next time you see a baby street walking elephant.

Lee Craker

5 RUMBLE IN THE JUNGLE

I awoke at 4 AM, quietly showered and packed my camera gear so as not to disturb my sleeping wife. I walked down the hill from our room at the Greater Mekong Lodge, crossed the highway and hiked up another steeper hill to the Anantara resort. At first light I hopped on a converted pickup truck used as a bus to take a few volunteers and workers to their residence, and then we continued on with a couple of mahouts to the plains and river where the elephants were quartered for the night. I was excited. An hour before sunrise there was a dense fog. Exactly what I had hoped for.

Waiting for the elephants in the morning fog to be brought by their mahouts to the river for a morning bath and refreshment I had time to reflect on this place called Anantara, and their mission. John Roberts had started The Golden Triangle Asian Elephant Foundation and Camp a few years back. His idea was to take elephants and mahouts off the streets and give them safe haven. Over time his ideas evolved and today he has a philosophy of leasing elephants and hiring their mahouts, while housing and feeding the mahout's families. The reason he leases the elephants is that he realized early on, that by purchasing an elephant it may encourage the mahout to just go out and get another elephant. So in John's mind instead of reducing the number of street elephants, purchasing an elephant could be contributing to the problem. I can see John's point. As I mentioned earlier money is the main motivating factor for most things in Thailand. If you buy an elephant, what is to keep the owner from buying two more with the profit? And if you buy those two, what is to keep him from buying four? And we already know where these elephants come from.

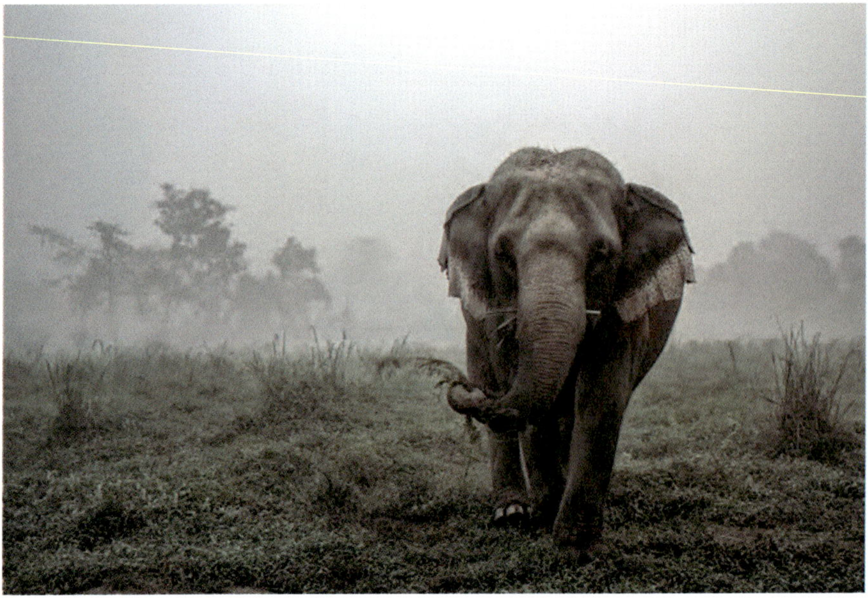

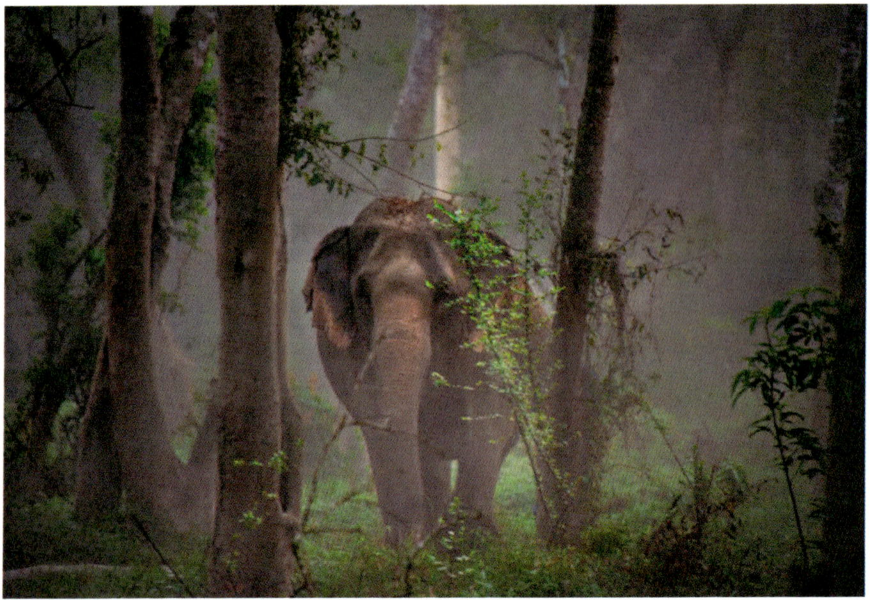

There are few good ideas that do not have a down side. The down side in John leasing elephants is that he does not own them, and therefore a mahout may chose to leave and return to the street, or in the case of one mahout I know of, leave in favor of breeding the elephant. Baby elephants broken and ready to work can bring a million baht ($32,000 U.S.). That is a great deal of money in Thailand.

John is also resolved to not exploiting the elephants at Anantara. Elephants enjoy a vast open area to roam by a refreshing river. Rides are only given bareback, but most guest interaction is on foot, or from the observation deck at the resort's excellent restaurant, where an elephant and mahout join the guests for breakfast.

Anantara's was a good place to start my investigation. John is one of a very few elephant rescue experts; he is dedicated, trying hard to ending abuse, and he is moving in the right direction. I can recommend Anantara's hotel and resort as a good place to go for responsible elephant tourism without any hesitation.

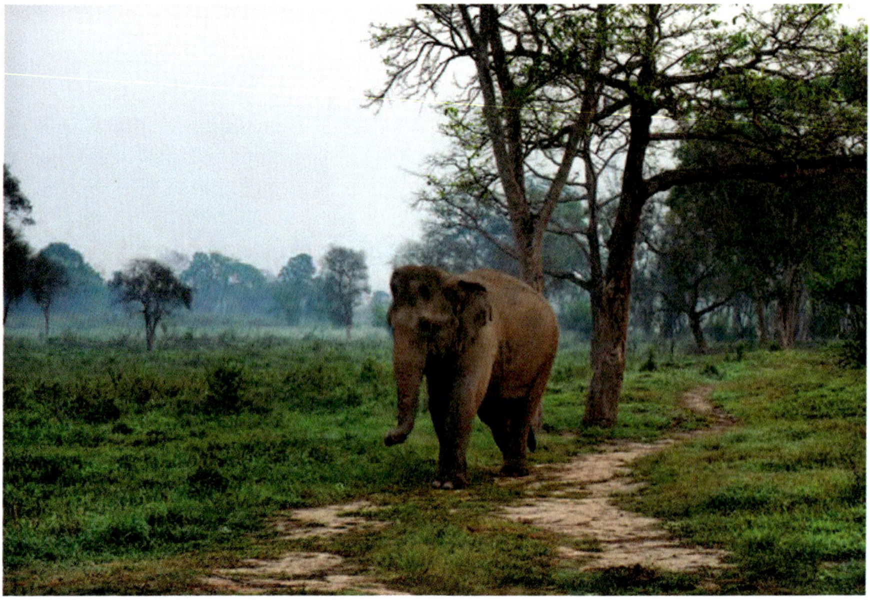

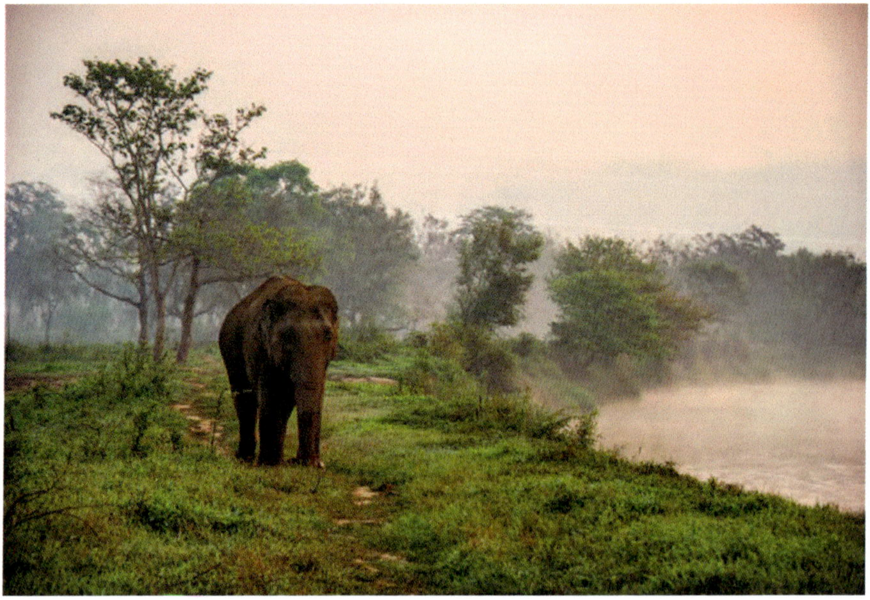

The Last Elephant

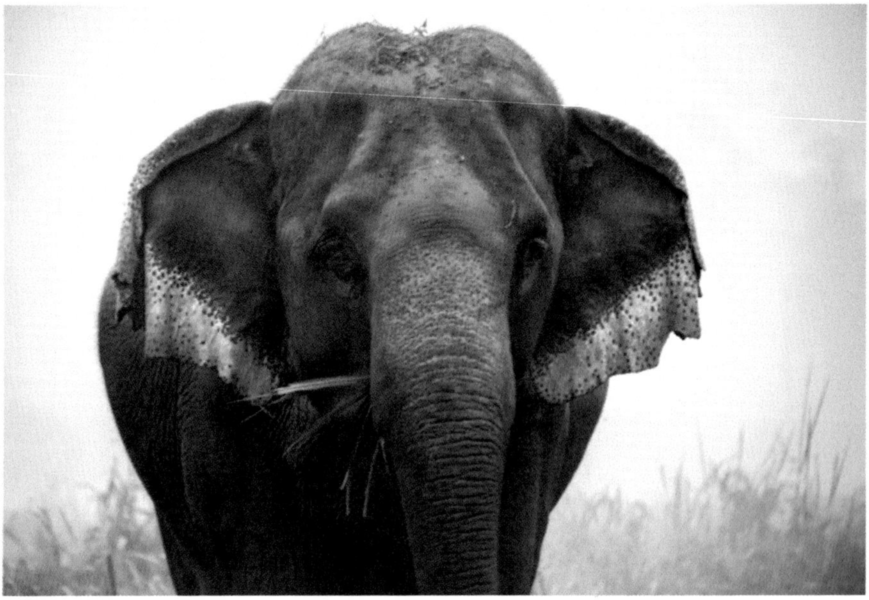

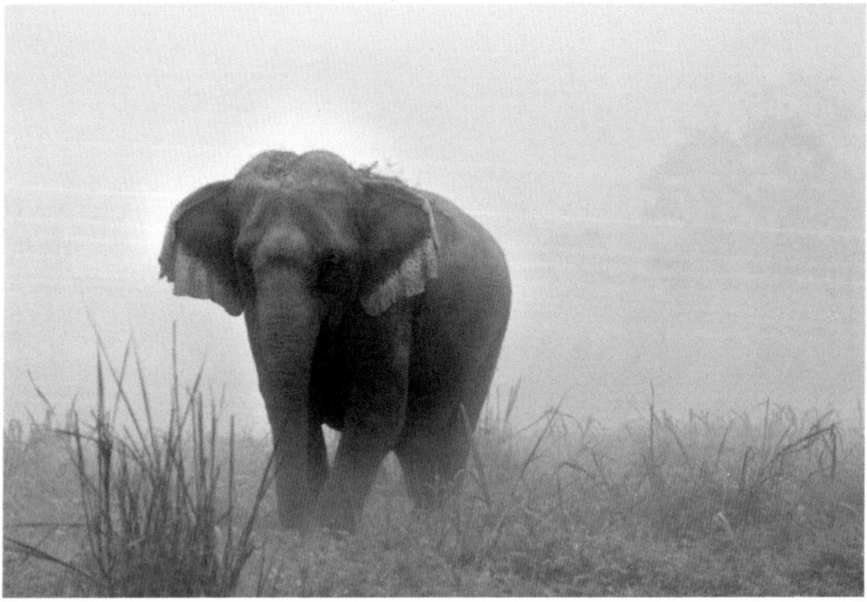

The Last Elephant

Lee Craker

6 MAESA ELEPHANT CAMP

Maesa Elephant Camp was the second camp I visited on my journey of exploration in North Thailand. Maesa was one of the camps that discontinued all correspondence when I told them I was a documentary photographer. So today I packed two cameras instead of one. I arrived at the camp with my wife early in the morning and was one of the first to enter the grounds when the gates opened at 9 AM. Most times I try not to have an agenda when reporting, but sometimes the facts are too overwhelming not have an opinion before the shoot. This was one of those times. In Chiang Mai there were many billboards and smaller advertisements for Maesa Elephant Camp, most used the words rescue and conservation, most also showed photos of elephants painting and playing football. When you know what exploitation is and see a photo of it along with the words rescue and conservation, it gets the juices flowing.

I was not disappointed. After we paid at the gate we were directed to a part of the camp where elephant rides were being given. I observed elephants, even smaller ones, being fitted with huge wooden seats that would carry tourists for a jaunt through the jungle. The tourists loved it. Mahouts were helping the people take souvenir photos of themselves on elephant taxi. That was the thing that would bother me the most this day, not the abuse itself, but the fact that the tourists were totally unaware of what they were contributing to. This day more than any other would give me the conviction to write this book. I looked around and saw the smiles and the joy people were experiencing totally unaware of the pain that the elephants have suffered through capture and learning to preform these unnatural acts.

We left the tower where the rides were being given and were encouraged to go and see the baby elephant. We walked to another part of the camp virtually alone as it was still early before the tourist busses arrived. I came across an open field where a mahout was teaching an elephant to paint. I walked in and observed for a few minutes. The process of elephant painting is that the mahout tugs on the elephant's ear in the direction he wants the elephant to paint. So it's actually mahout painting, but shhhh that's a secret. This day the elephant was having trouble finishing the painting, and the tugs were getting hard. Using my wife as translator the mahout said that people were not supposed to see this part of the show, and would I not take photos and please leave. He was a very nice young man, almost all Thais are, so I thanked him very much and we left. How many people in the world believe an elephant paints? I was told that when they came up with the idea elephant paintings toured the world and are in a few famous galleries. I don't know how much of that is true, but it is a shame that the mahout gets no credit (or money) for his unusual artistry.

After we observed mahout painting we continued down the trail to where the baby elephant was kept. Baby elephants have a universal appeal. It's easy to see why a baby elephant can bring a million baht. The babies can turn large profits for those that own them, I know, because my wife made many trips to the little booth beside the cage to purchase bananas to feed the young elephant. It was very cute that the baby elephant did not eat the bananas, but instead fed them to it's mother. The scene reminded me of my own four year old that will ask mom for a snack then run over to dad and feed me the treat.

The Last Elephant

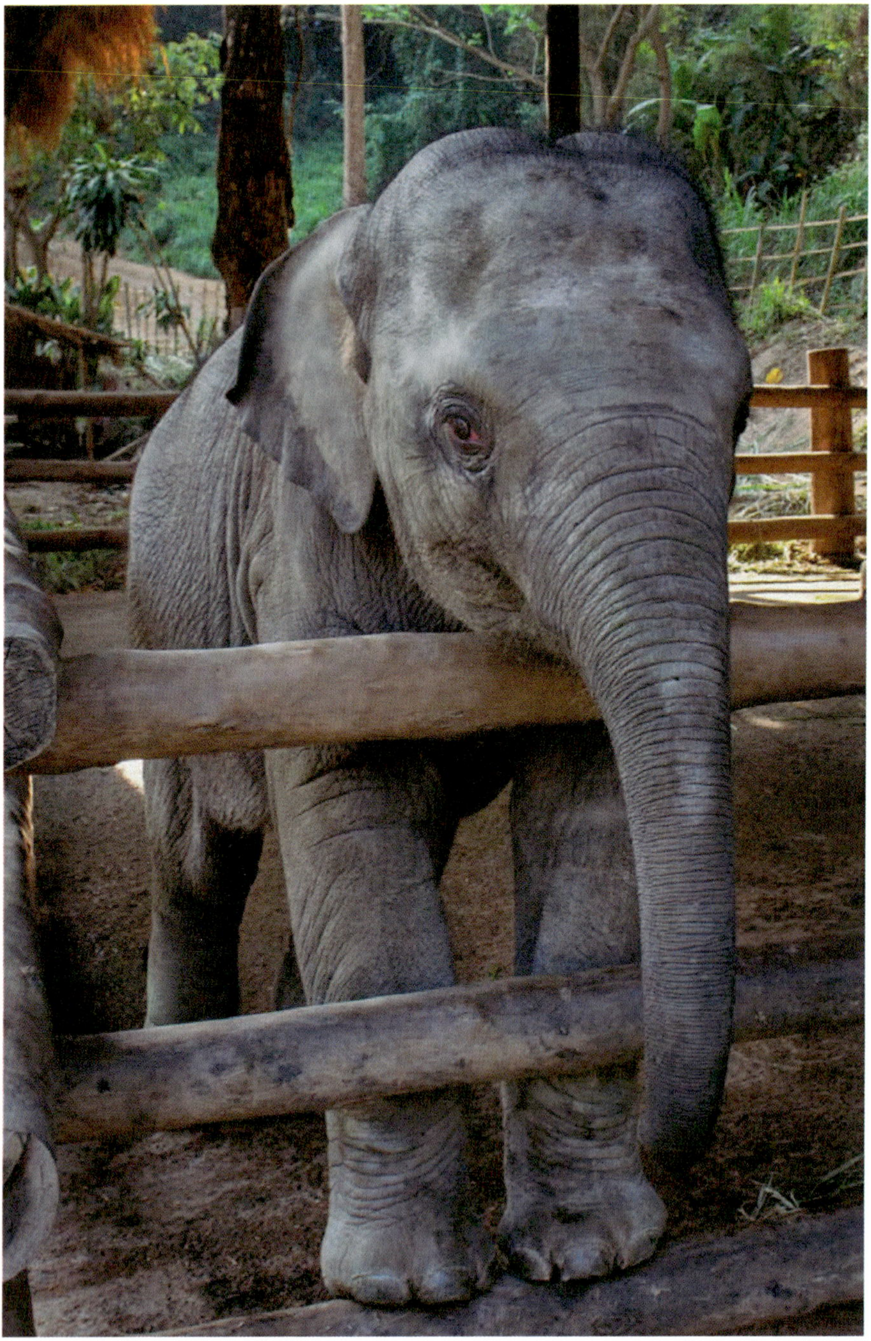

After visiting the baby elephant it was time to head up to the area where the elephant show was held. The show was put on in a large arena that reminded me of how a western rodeo is laid out. A large open area surrounded by covered stands that could hold about 1500 spectators. Today it was nearly filled to capacity. The parking lot was filled with many tour busses bringing patrons that had signed up for a tour of the attractions near Chiang Mai, of which Maesa Camp was one. The show included almost every elephant act I had come to believe was abusive and elephant exploitation. There was mahout painting, elephant dancing, football, basketball, and a variety of other tricks the elephants had been taught.

Maesa has a large sign near the entrance that lists the names with photos of the 83 resident elephants they have "rescued". The elephants have been saved from street begging or logging operations only to end up living on a small tract of land or in cages and have been retrained to perform for large numbers of tourists which lines the pockets of the owners of Maesa Elephant Camp with the Thai gold we hear so much about.

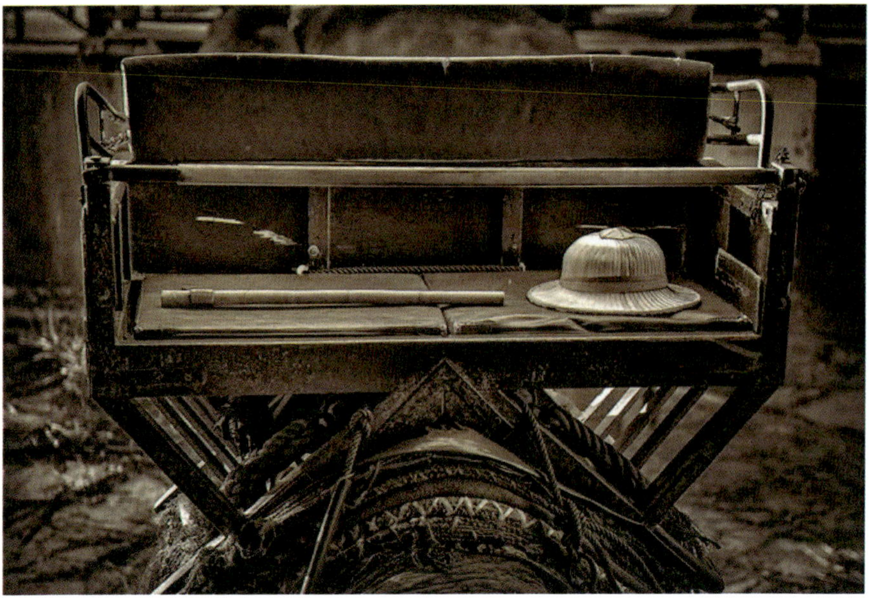

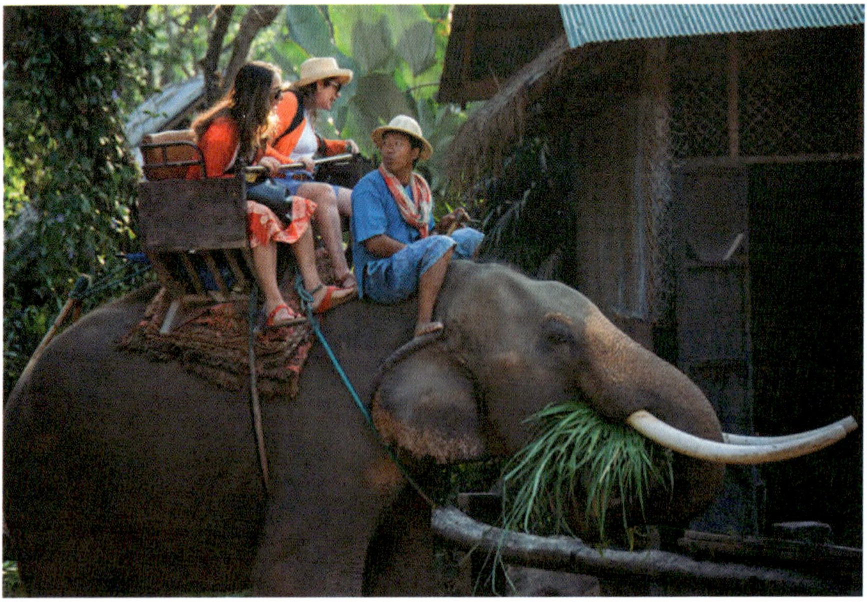

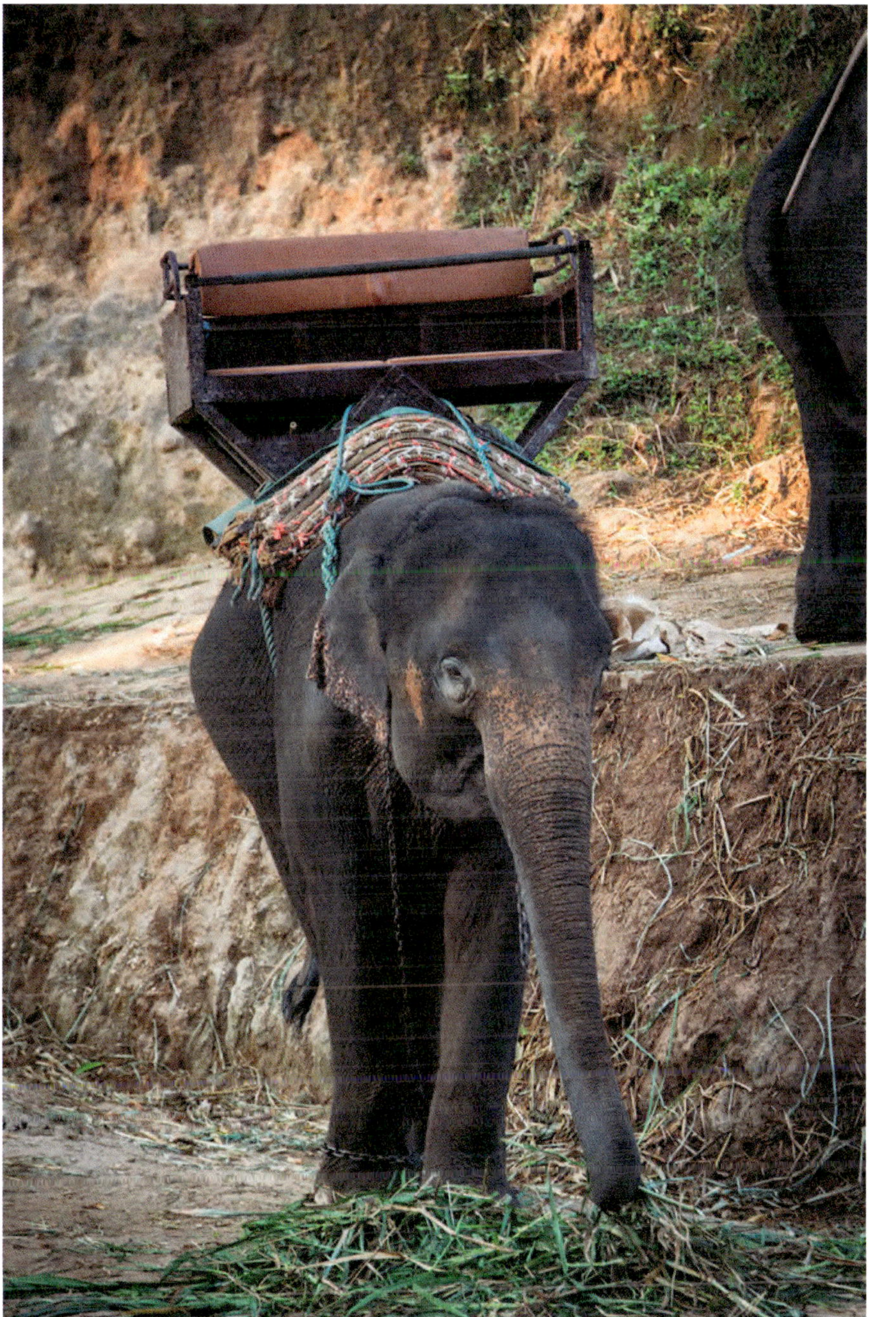

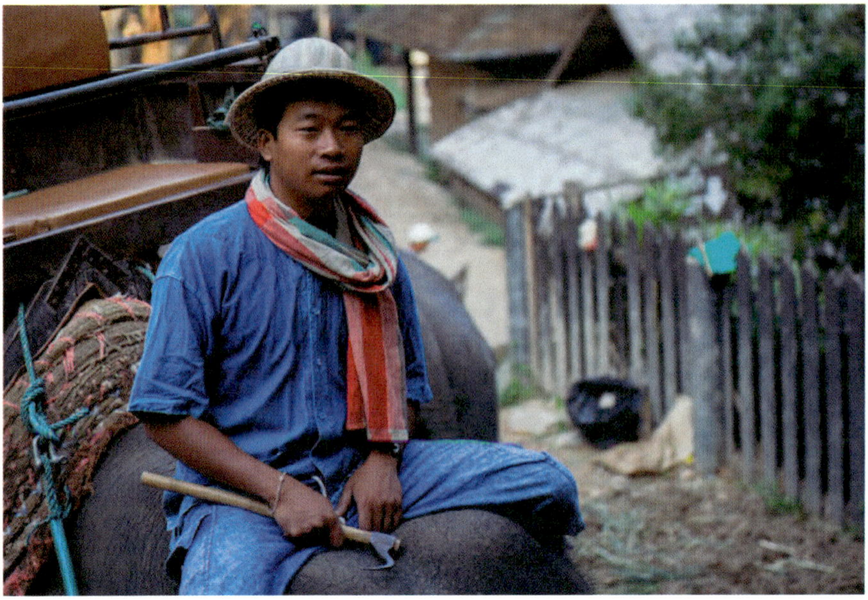

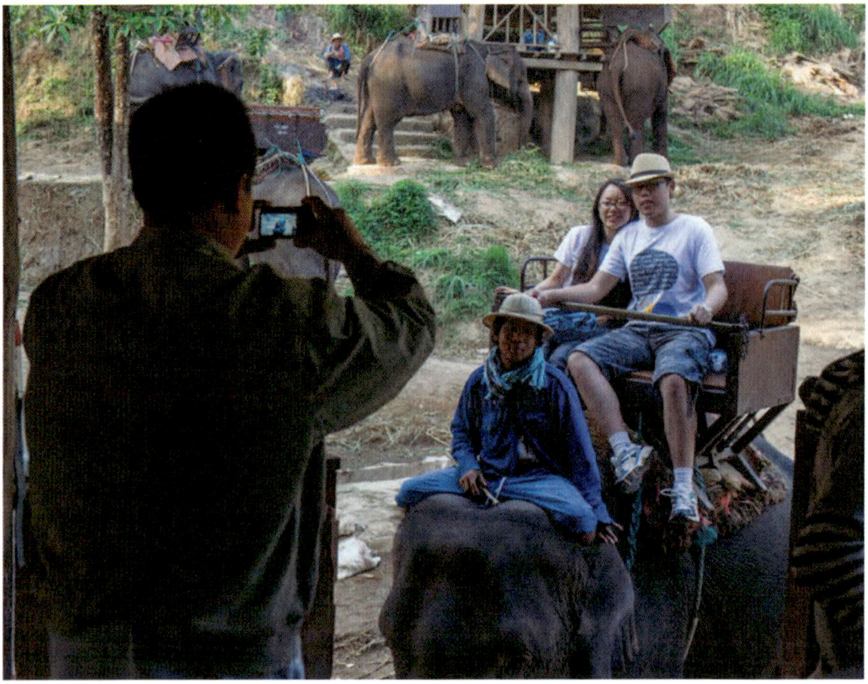

The Last Elephant

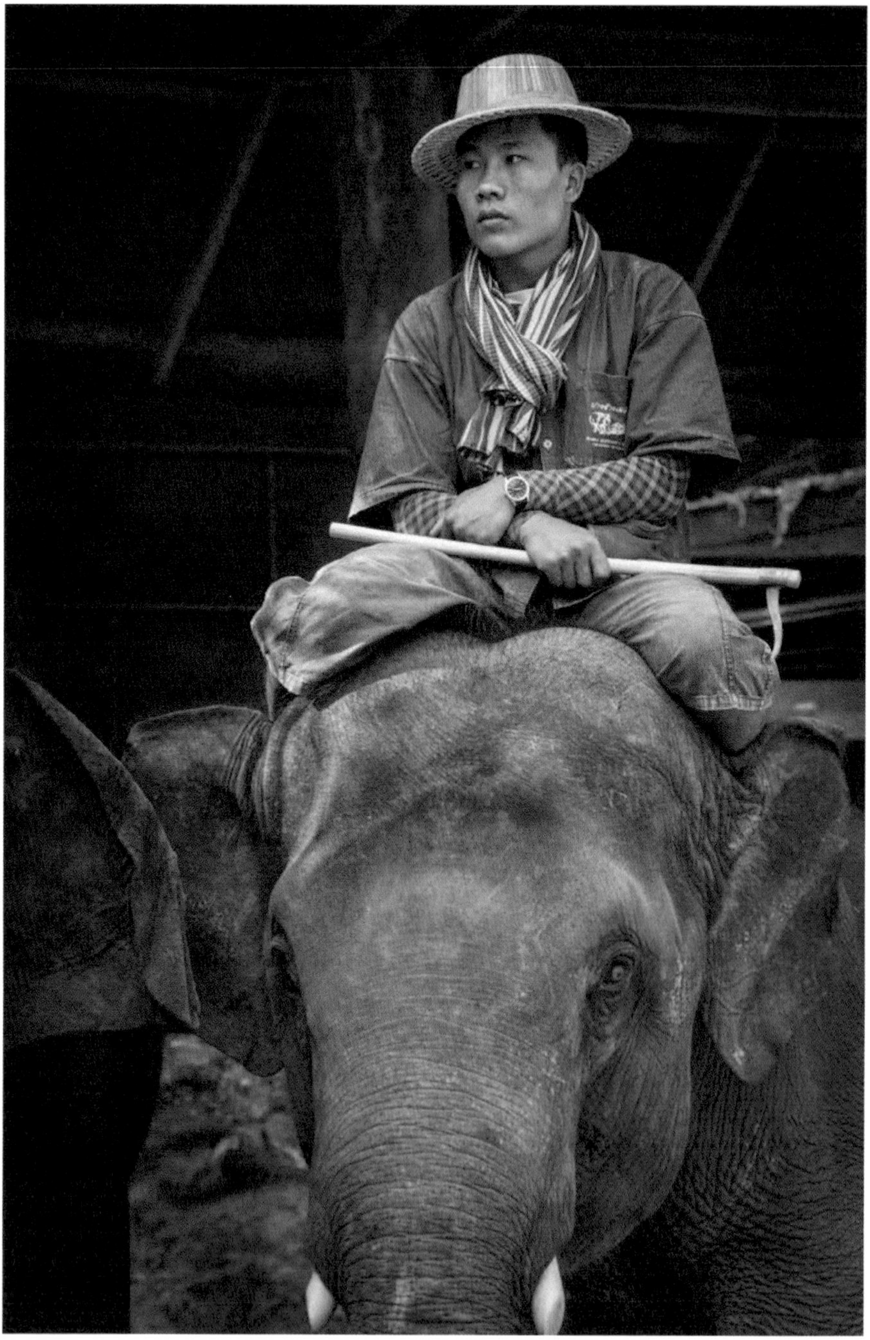

The Last Elephant

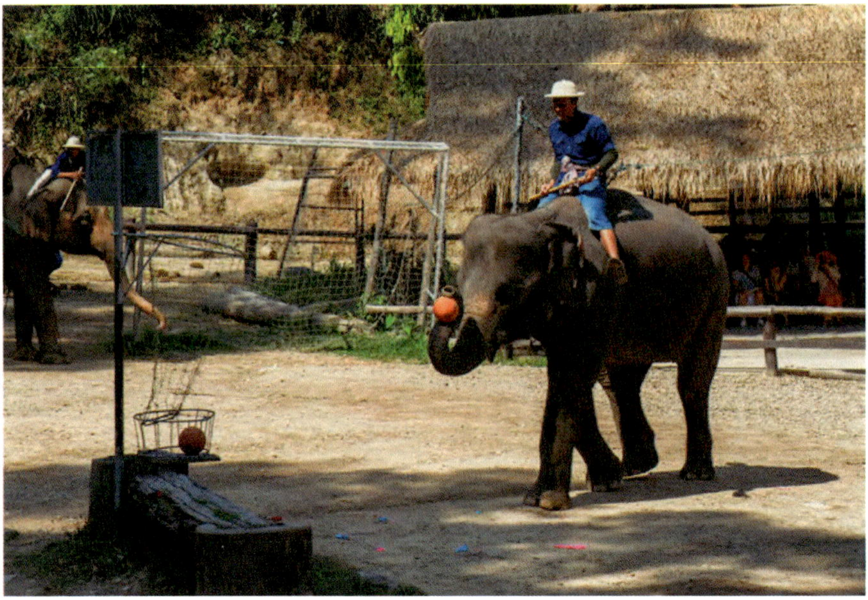

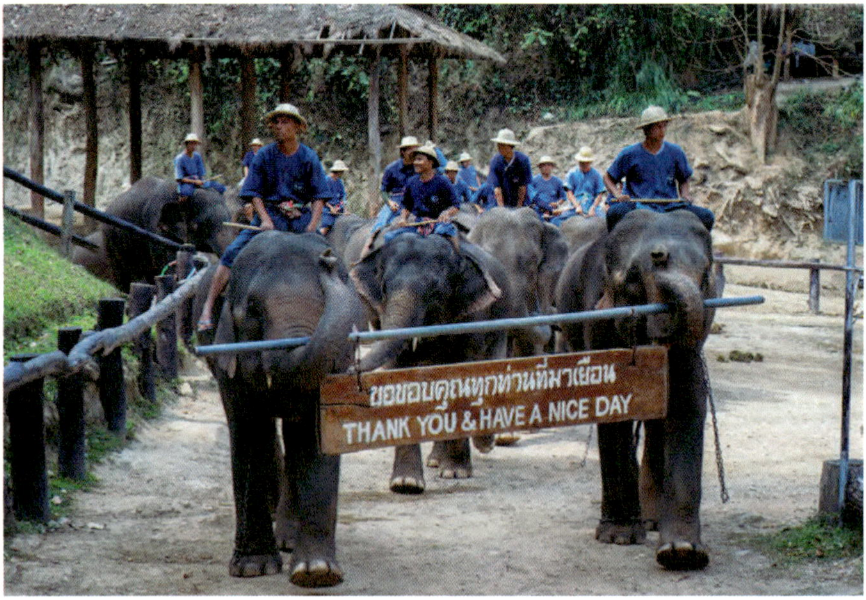
ขอขอบคุณทุกท่านที่มาเยือน
THANK YOU & HAVE A NICE DAY

Obviously I did not have the opportunity to interview anyone at Maesa. I observed the things that go on at Maesa as a tourist. My photos speak for themselves.

There are hundreds of camps like Maesa in Thailand; they exist because tourists support them. The most powerful weapons we have to fight against elephant abuse are money and information. If you disagree with elephant abuse do not support camps that abuse elephants, and spread the word to others. Without our money these camps will disappear.

7 THE CHIANG MAI ZOO

What can you say about a zoo? Even the word has a derogatory meaning. "This place is a zoo". Zoos are a holdover from another time. A time when big game hunting was popular and Teddy Roosevelt carried a big stick. Most zoos today donate funds to wildlife conservation in an attempt to improve their image. That is kind of like cigarette companies supporting cancer research. Zoos come from a time when people felt the only way to experience a wild animal was in a cage. Some zoos today are in the process of expanding and converting to a nature park type of experience. This can only happen in areas with a vast expanse of land. It takes 3 acres to support one elephant properly. This can never happen in a city. We have evolved, and technology has given us vast, and better, resources to educate our children about wildlife. How educational is a wild animal in a cage? Wouldn't it be better to support the growth of better real nature parks and let our children see the wildlife in their natural habitat? All this is idealistic, but I truly wish my home state of Colorado would have had the foresight to preserve natural habitat, for today there is very little to be found. Zoos need to go away in favor of a better experience, and elephants should never be in a zoo.

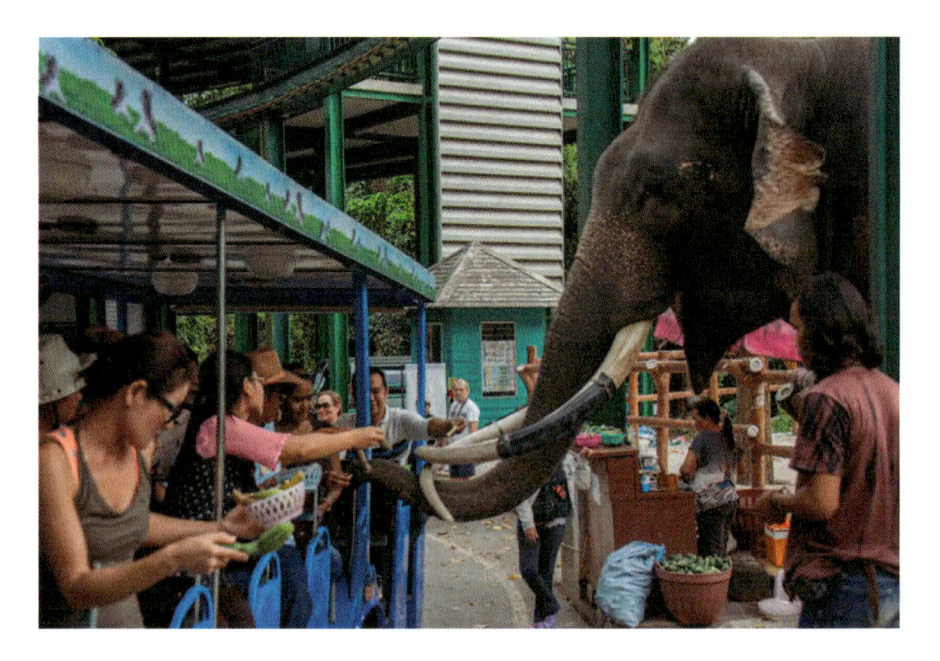

The Last Elephant

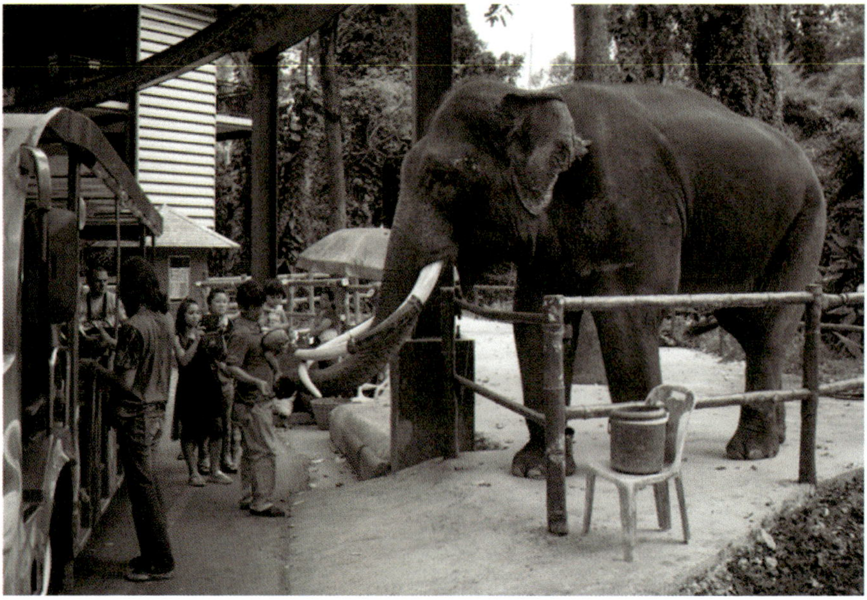

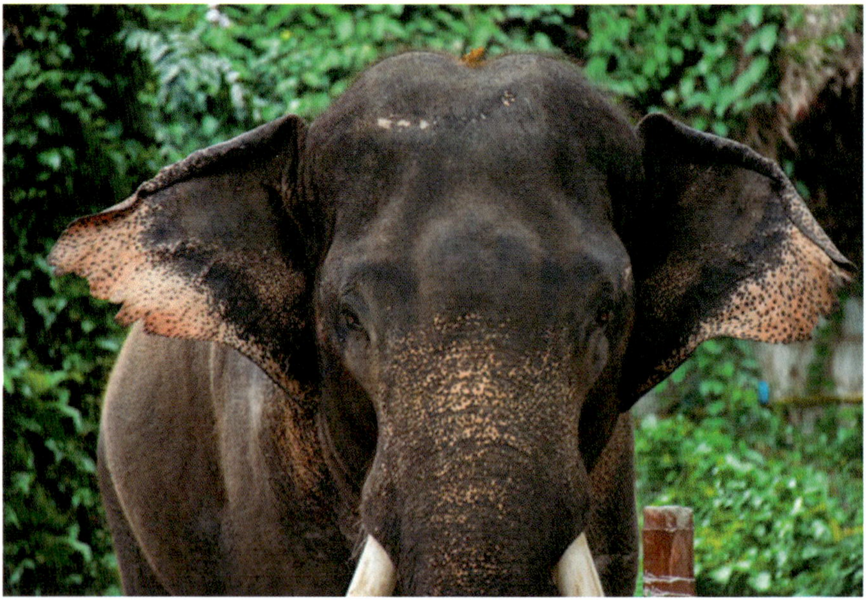

The Last Elephant

8 ELEPHANT NATURE PARK / LEK CHAILERT

Lek Chailert *is* Elephant Nature Park and Save Elephant Foundation. This petite Thai woman from a modest hill tribe background is a one-woman army in the fight to save the elephants of Thailand (and everywhere else). As a young woman she watched the logging operations near her hill tribe home. She saw and experienced the pain of the elephants first hand. She said *"I saw the pain in the elephants eyes, and I went home, but I could never get that elephant eye out of my mind"*. She spent what little money she had for medicine to help the injured elephants, and found others who would help her. Lek's love for the elephants and her desire to help them led to her starting Elephant Nature Park where she is able to rescue and care for elephants and give them a safe haven. Her enemies, those who would continue to capture, torture and abuse elephants are powerful and influential people. These people try to shut her operation down, threaten to block her websites, yet she continues to fight for the elephants she loves, and does so in a soft spoken humble manner. She fully understands the intricacies of the elephant trade. More than once she said to me "This is a complex business". The complexities range from bureaucrats and big business tycoons to poor hill tribe people, who are pawns in the game, trying to eek out a marginal living by capturing and training elephants.

The Last Elephant

Elephant Nature park was the last stop on my tour of North Thailand. It had been a long three weeks. No longer could I share the excitement of the other passengers in the van at the prospect of seeing an elephant, I had seen and interacted with elephants almost every day for the past three weeks. I had seen good, and I had seen bad, and those experiences had prepared me for what I was about to encounter.

I had a full day and night to learn about and enjoy the camp before my interview with Lek, which gave me a great opportunity to see what this camp was all about. This was the camp that had said in an e-mail "we are the best", I wanted to find out why.

We were shown to our quarters which was a small cabin built in a rustic thatched hut style. The room was nice, but basic. There was a refrigerator, floor air conditioner and TV, however, there was no television or phone reception, there was a mosquito net surrounding the comfortable bed that reminded me of an old Bob Hope movie, "Call Me Bwana" I was told there was Wi-Fi in parts of the camp, but I never found a hot spot. I actually did not try that hard to find the internet, I found it relaxing to be away from the modern world for a couple of days. The majority of visitors who come to ENP are back packers, young people on a budget, a stark contrast from the upscale Anantara's Golden Triangle Resort. The guest cottages are located near the main group of buildings that serve as an information center, banana warehouse and dining hall. The meals are strictly vegetarian, and served buffet style. The community dining room also serves as a 2nd story raised observation deck, open on 3 sides with a protective railing and safety zone so the elephants can be fed goodies of bananas and vegetables by the guests

After the accommodations, the first thing I noticed that was different than the other camps was that no one was riding an elephant. Not the mahouts, not the guests, no one. Also I did not see the mahouts carrying Bullhooks to control the elephants. I had the opportunity to ask Diana Edelman, an American who assists Lek, about this during a tour of the camp. She told me that Bullhooks were not allowed, if a mahout was caught using a Bullhook they would be warned and if caught a second time they would be fired. Being fired in Thailand is a very big deal. Thailand is an impoverished county and being out of work makes a hard life, an impossible life. I asked about riding the elephants, and a mahout told me that is also forbidden. Lek's philosophy is to allow elephants as much as possible, to just be elephants. No work, no rides, no shows, just elephants hanging out with other elephants.

During my stay I saw first hand another large problem elephants face. Slash and burn is what it is called when the forest is burned to make way for planting crops. Slash and burn has significantly reduced the natural habitat of wild elephants, and while I was at the park, at times the thick smoke rolled over the valley like a fog.

The Last Elephant

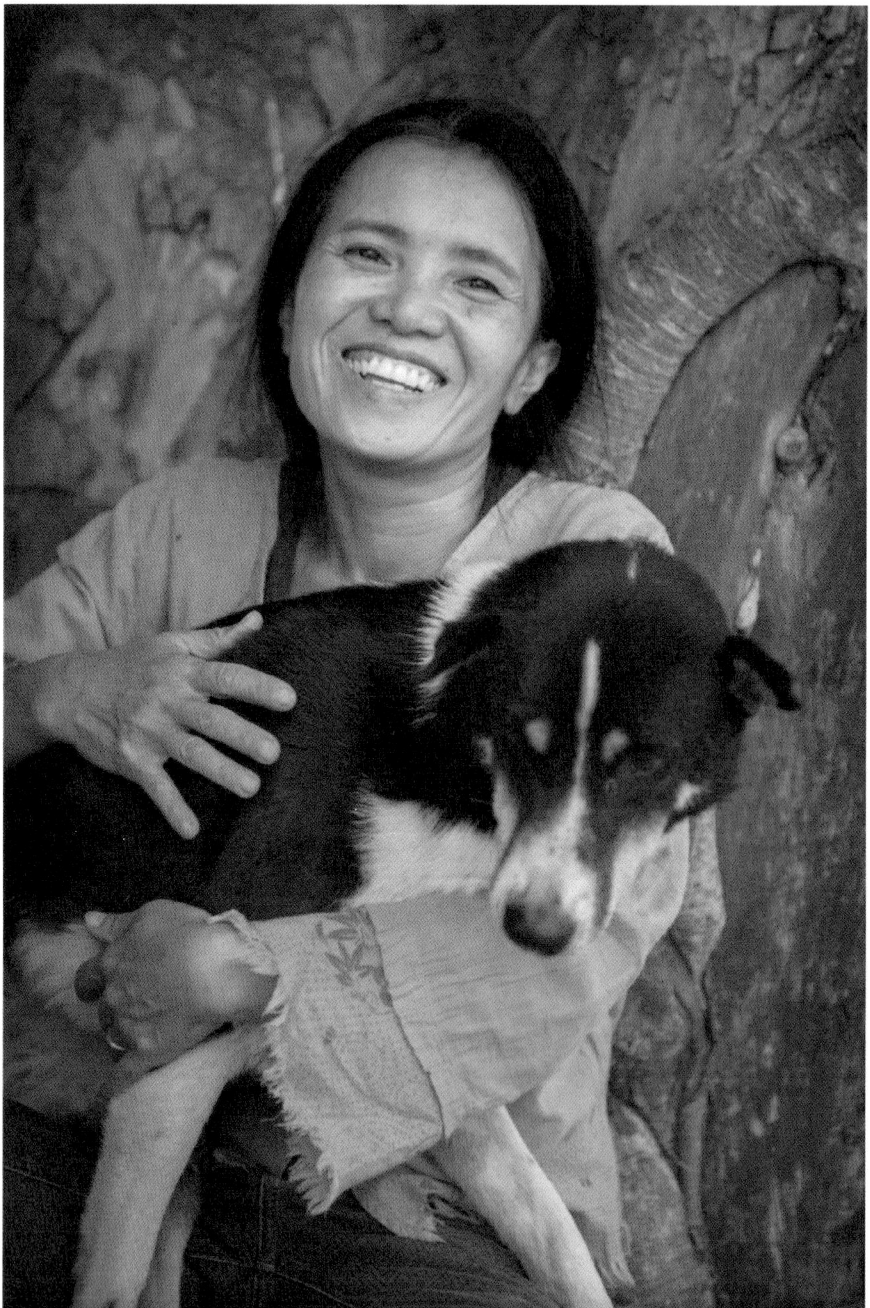

Lek's philosophy is indeed rather unique. The argument that most quote "*rescue*" camps use is that the elephant shows and elephant rides generate funds so they can support the elephants, who can eat up to 440 lb. of food a day. To the novice and most tourists this seems to make sense. It takes money to support elephants. So how does Lek's camp generate the necessary funds? Well, it takes more work. Lek is very active in fundraising and education. Also amazingly, she is able to charge the people who come and volunteer at her camp for the privilege of cleaning up elephant poo. This is called responsible tourism, ecotourism if you will. Responsible tourism is only a small niche in the tourist business today, but with any luck it will be the wave of the future. There is a small but growing group of people that believe holidays are more enjoyable if along with sightseeing you try to make the world a little better place to live in. In my mind Lek's model is important to look at. Lek is proving to Thailand and the world that greed need not be the prime motivation in the elephant trade, putting animal welfare first can and does work. To be fair, John Roberts has exactly the same business philosophy, in a slightly different business model. Both of these models are to be applauded and supported.

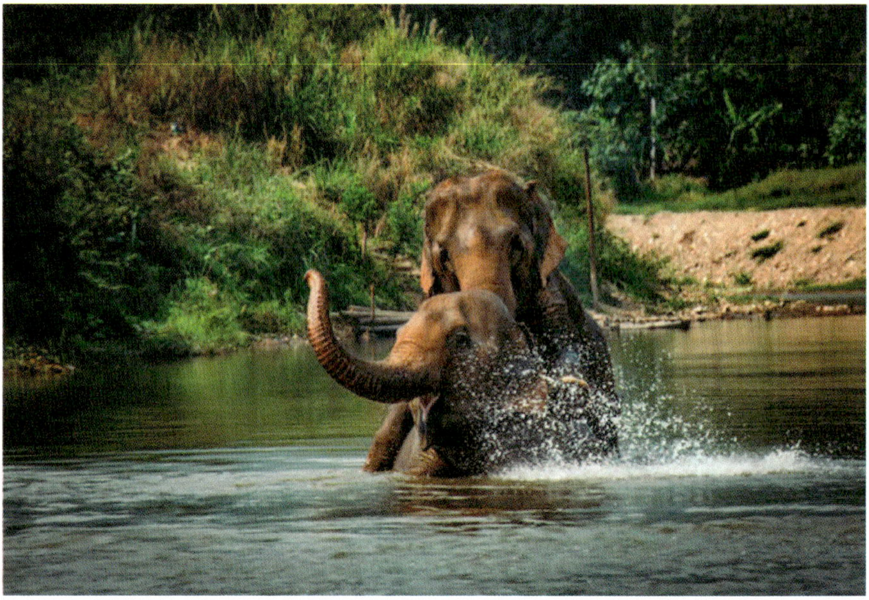

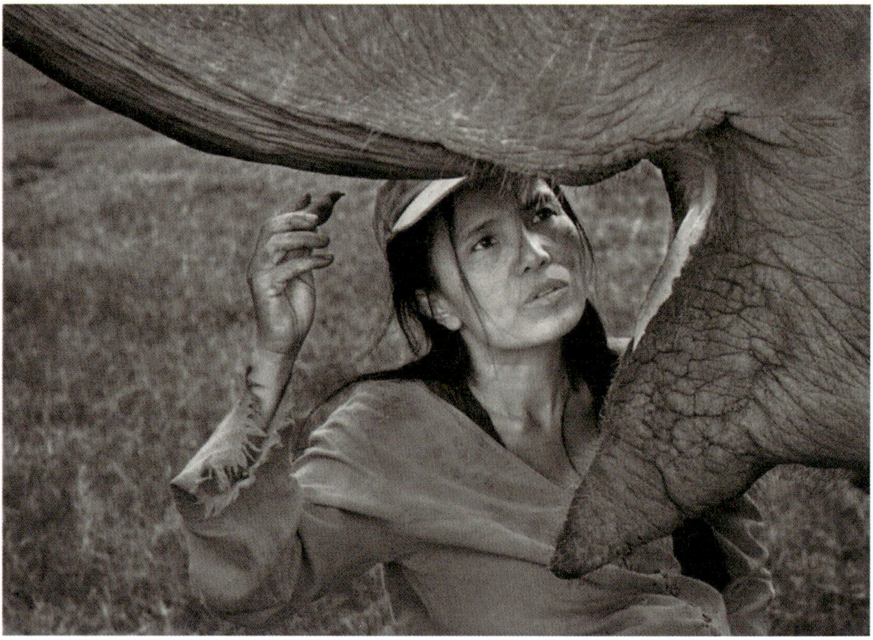

The Last Elephant

Lee Craker

The Last Elephant

9 HOW TO HELP THE ELEPHANTS

At the end of four weeks I boarded a plane in Chiang Rai bound for Bangkok where I would catch a train and head home to rural Thailand. There was much to think about. In just four weeks I had gone from complete elephant novice to a concerned advocate, and I was on elephant abuse overload. I had elephant park brain fry. I had made over three thousand photos and recorded several hours of audio. I had talked to several major players in the fight to save elephants and seen their work. I had also seen the other end of the spectrum. It would take time to process my thoughts, sort through the images and listen to the audio. Time was on my side, this was, and is not, a breaking news story. So over the next few months I collected my thoughts, and talked with my friends about how we could best address these issues. Our game plan changed several times. We knew if our efforts were to be successful, or at least have an impact on the problem, people must be made aware of the issues before they come to Thailand, before their first encounter with a cute street walking baby elephant. We want to encourage people to come to Thailand, but as responsible tourists. At first we thought of a book, a sort of a Thailand elephant travel guide that would educate people planning to come to Thailand. That sounded good at first but then we realized that the book would need to continually be revised as camps made changes in their philosophies, and became more open (we hope) to responsible tourism. We also realized we needed to be comprehensive. My travels were to North Thailand, but tourists visit everywhere in Thailand with the most popular areas being Bangkok and the southern resort areas. These popular areas are teaming with street begging elephants and elephant camps, which are continually changing their operations. Revising a book 3 or 4 times a year would be impractical, and costly.

A functional intuitive website would be the most practical approach. The website would be free to the user, which is important. People would be free to contribute financially to the project if they wanted, but the cost of information would not cost a dime. The website could also have user input, allow user ratings of camps, let people upload images and through forums we could allow lively discussions so people with differing views and philosophies could have their voices heard. A website would address our major goal, education. The weapon that will defeat elephant abuse and ensure the survival of the elephant species is education. The pen is mightier than the Bullhook, more powerful than the crush. I'm happy to say that as I write this, a website is in the planning stages, and on hold until proper funding is available.

By purchasing this book you have already contributed to this process. You have already helped to set the wheels in motion. For that we thank you. We only ask that you don't stop. If you believe in the cause, tell others. Let your voice be heard, as loudly and clearly as a trumpeting elephant in the forest.

Can one person make a difference? I give you John Roberts, Dan Bucknell, and Lek Chailert. Each started alone with a dream. Each has made Thailand and our world a better place. There are others, and you can add your name to that list. Helping is so easy. All it takes is talking to others about the problems and solutions. The power to change what is wrong is in the hands of those who visit Thailand. Responsible tourism and a concerned public will put an end to the crush. All I ask is that you use the power you already have, one Dollar, one Yen and one Baht at a time.

Thank you for taking the time to read this and helping the elephants. More information and ways to help can be found on our blog here: http://www.leecraker.com/wp/saving-elephants

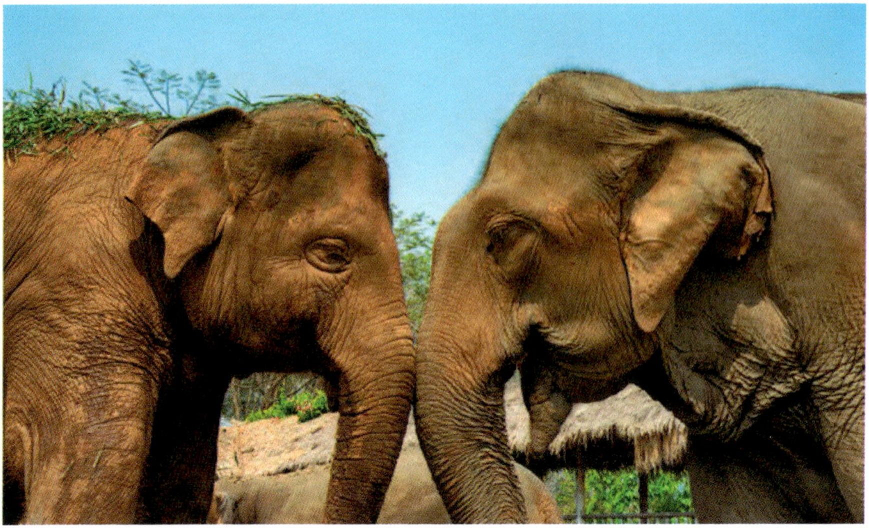

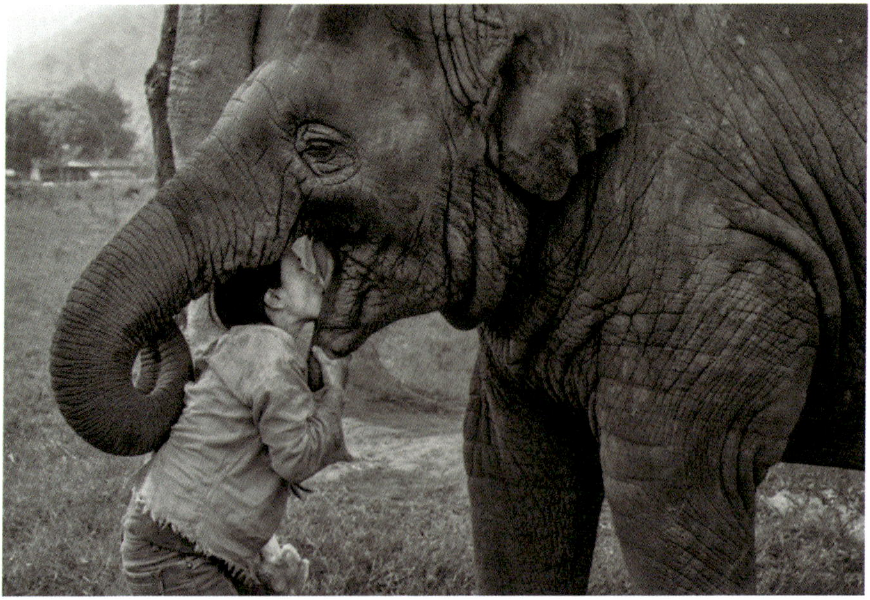

The Last Elephant

There is a saying in Thailand, "Up to You"
Is this the last elephant? – Up to you.